Poetic Hauntings- Oddities and Entities from a Darkly Creative Soul

Luke Mayo

BookLeaf Publishing

India | USA | UK

Presentation by *BookLeaf Publishing*

Web: www.bookleafpub.com

E-mail: info@bookleafpub.com

ISBN: 9789360949488

First edition 2024

I dedicate this book to every person who reads it. I hope that, whoever you are, and whatever darkness you face, you are able to confront and overcome that darkness in all its forms.

ACKNOWLEDGEMENT

I've known emotional and practical darkness throughout my life, and I've had so many people who've helped me to face that darkness. These are the people I thank in these acknowledgements.

To list every person I want to thank by name would fill a world full of books. I will therefore cover the groups of people I acknowledge in the broadest possible terms.

Every public service and charitable organization I've worked and volunteered for deserves my praise and gratitude for shaping my life and creative voice. The material they've given me for my poetry has been immeasurable.

Renew Counselling was there for me during some of the darker times in my life, and they helped me to get through them. In a world which questions the need for and place of counselling and therapy, I can testify that counselling is amazing if done properly, which Renew does.

University of Suffolk welcomed me onto their undergrad and postgrad courses in English and Creative and Critical Writing. This has forged my passion for poetry, and empowered me to follow that passion. I'm so proud to be an alumnus of this university.

Lastly, and probably mostly, I thank my family. Literally every day and every step of my life, good and bad, they've been by my side helping me through it. Every person in every one of these groups, for better or worse, has helped me along my life, and therefore enabled the poetry in this book, which is based to a large extent on my life experiences.

Thank you all so much.

PREFACE

Those of us who have spent any amount of time in the real world will know that the real world can be a dark, scary place. Finding a way to navigate this dark, scary place can be a challenge. I promise you that doing it right, and doing it well, is worth it.

For me, creative writing is a massive part of navigating the world's darkness. This effectively explains the existence of this book. The poetry you'll find in the pages that follow are the result of my contemplations about the wonderfully dark world we live in.

By writing poetry and following my creative passions, I aim to make the world a little bit lighter. I hope this goes some way to making your world lighter, too.

Thank you for reading, and sharing this journey with me.

The Lonely Lurker

I'm waiting for you
I crave your presence
I yearn for a friendship
I'll stop at nothing until I get it

In the shadows
In the gentle but chilling breeze
In the creaks of floorboards
That's where I am
Lying in wait

I'm on the hunt for one thing
You know what it is
The one thing to satiate me

A text back
Literally
That's all I want
Is it too much to ask?
You keep ignoring me
Not a single reply
I mean honestly
It's a bit rude

Just one text back, yeah?

Promise?
Cheers, mate

Childhood Days, Childhood Friends

Ours was a firm friendship
Pure and true
You're not here anymore
Your memory shines still

You soothed an anxiety-riddled soul
You kept my nights company
You guarded me as I slept
You greeted me of many a morning

You were my stalwart ally
My faithful companion
My childhood buddy
The lonely pangs of daily boyhood
You diminished them with daily friendship
My gratitude is forever yours

Your departure
Eventual and inevitable
Distant and sobering
The herald of adulthood
A life without you

You were taken to a toyshop

Ready for another child's playtime
Whoever they may be
They're lucky to have you

You were never just a stuffed toy rabbit
You were my Thumper
Your soft, fluffy ears
Your plush heart and soul
They live within me

Hellbound Valley of Night Demons

Night is not my time for rest
Sleep comes not with ease
No counting sheep works for my ravaged mind

My inner demons
Mocking me with hellish visions

Sometimes it's living mannequins taunting me
Sometimes it's mangled corpses of gore
Sometimes it's inescapable dread
Sometimes it's people from my past who despise
me

Open my eyes and the visions vanish
Sleep brings them crawling back
The demons lie waiting in my very soul
These creatures and their visions are a part of me
No escape
No release
No respite
Just demons and their games

We are destined to do battle
With a positive spirit I might win

I'll claim victory one day

Liberation of the Mind

You used to come for me
I was your favourite and easiest target
You hurt me and bruised me
Twisted my mind and broke my heart
Years of my life taken by you
All because I let you do it

Not any more
It stops now
I'm protecting myself
Shielding from you
Escaping your control
I deserve better

I'm no longer your puppet
I'm no longer your slave
I'm no longer your plaything
I'm no longer your punchbag
I'm no longer yours

I'm free to be me
I will live my life
I will do good things
Because I can
Because you can't stop me

Because I'm not yours to control

You chose to push me away
Good luck in the life you've chosen
My life will be fine without you
And that's a promise

Blank Page, Blank Life

My life is the story
I write with what I do
But now the pages are empty
Just like my ideas

All I've done so far
The adventures I've written
I've come to a pause now
I've had pauses before
Sometimes it leads to a chapter break
Sometimes a story ends to begin another

The choice is mine

I don't know what I'll do
I could do anything
Meet new characters
Explore new settings
Or rest a while

Either way
The blank page won't defeat me
I'll overcome it
Write with a little magic
A little sparkle

A little fun

The blank page
It doesn't need to be a blank life

The Nobody Man

Have you seen him?
Most likely
You just don't know it

He keeps to the outskirts of periphery vision
Wandering the paths of uncanny valley

We see him all
We notice him not
We know him never
He knows us forever

He walks alongside us
Accompanies our every move
Watches our every action
Keeps a mental note

Who is this man?
What does he know?
Why is he here?
What has he been through?
How long has he been around?
How much longer will he stay?
What's it all for?

Knowing the answer
Might be worse than not knowing

Living Bereavement

You sit beside me
But you're not you
You're a testament to life lived
But you're not here

All that life lived
All those memories
Drifting down the river of neurological decay

The heroic deeds you achieved
They stand with validity yet
The many souls you love
They return your years of adoration
Even if you don't remember them

My tears for you
They're happy and sad
Happy that you're here before me
My stalwart hero
Sad that you don't know me
Nor who you are to me
Nor who I am to you

Your life and character are amazing

Your mind took them both away and left you
behind
I mourn your loss in your very presence

Your memories depart
Your legacy remains
I live my life as a tribute to yours

Love's Greatest Sacrifice Imaginable

I love you so much
There's nothing I wouldn't do for you
I'll even do the hardest thing
Let you love someone else

We were childhood friends
I kept you company
I stood by you in your loneliness
We gave each other joy in life's miserable
landscape

You were my reason for everything
You were my everything
But no more
For now you've found another
A companion whose love is true
A solid groundwork for a lifetime of devotion

I love you so much
It doesn't matter that you no longer love me
back
I love you so much
I'll accept that your happiness leads you away
from me

I love you so much
I'll let my existence fade if it assures your future

I won't be there to see that future
I was privileged to be in your past
Your happiness is my priority
For I am your imaginary friend

Now you've found love in reality
I am bound by duty and love to let you go
Sad satisfaction is my eternal reward

Workless and Ethicless

Youth of today
Born into a world requiring work
A world and requirement they reject

"Work is sick and twisted"
"Work is the matrix"
"We demand change"
"We'll overthrow the system"

Seriously?

Survival requires work
Achievement requires work
Bounty requires work
Success requires work

No work?
No value
Goodbye to all you care about
The good life floats beyond your grasp
Never to be seen again

Find a good purpose
Work hard and well for it
This is great

This is ethical
That's how legends are made

Or don't work at all
You'll be nothing at all, never

Mirror, Mirror

You look like me
But you're not me
You match my every physical detail
Like two porcelain dolls
Like two card decks

But that's where the resemblance ends

You don't have my life
My experiences
My memories
My soul
You don't have my friendships
My loves
My heartbreaks
My loathings

What's mine is mine
It enriches my life
I look at your identical face
I see all that's missing

I can't help wondering
What if you take my life?
Steal my identity and escape into the night?

Replace me in all things?
Abandon me as the empty shell you are now?

Nobody would know
Maybe not even me
We could take turns at living
We might not even realise ourselves

It could be fun
It could be horrifying

The Things People Teach Us

People are like teachers
We learn so much from them

Things like
How to smile our face when our heart is sad
Things like
How to say "I'm fine" when we're not

Things like
How to stay in bad places
Things like
How to ignore our bad feelings

Things like
How to keep going when we don't want to
Things like
How to be quiet when our soul screams

Things like
How to cry without making a sound
Things like
How to take emotional blows in silent
anonymity

People teach us how to do it
But they never teach us why

Prisoner of my Mind's Cycle

The same interior dimensions
The same internal monologue
Words repeating and repeating

I'm worthless
I'm useless
I'm a failure
Round and round
Again and again
Always and forever

However fast I run
However far I go
I'm always the same inside
Never changing
Never escaping

Whatever I do
My mind's monologue is with me
Calling out to me from the shadows
Whispering through the silence

I wish for quiet
I'd love solitude
Peace and freedom are my dreams

None will be mine
The monologue hold me captive
I'm the prisoner of my mind's cycle

Those We Meet Once

I met you on the street
At the train station
In the shop

We shared a smile
Had a laugh
Offered friendly opinions and advice

Then you disappeared

I move on with my life
Journeying through each day
I think about you often
But you're not here

Who are you?
Where are you?
What life are you living?
Are you real?
Did I imagine you?
Are you asking the same questions of me?

So many people
Passing through my life
Appearing and disappearing

They rock off into a mystery
As I do for them

Where are we all going?
Is it the same place?
Will we meet again?

We'll see

Lovers and Leaches

If you see someone acting in friendship
Think once
Think twice
Keep your wits
The deadliest dangers come in disguise

Some people are the embodiments of love
Some people are good at faking it
Some people live for making the world better
Some people thrive on destruction
Some people thrive on self-empowerment
Some people blame others and run

How can you discern one from the other?
Just give it time

In good times and bad
In light moments and dark
People show you who they really are

Some people brave life's risks
Some people are worth risks
Some people expect risks from others
But they don't deserve it

We should always ask ourselves
Which one are we?

Fallen Heroes

Riddle me this
When do heroic acts lead to a villainous legacy?
When they're done for selfish and entitled
people

I tried because you asked me
I stood by you because you needed me
I supported you because you wanted me
I saved you because you were in danger

I did it gladly
Ongoing heroism
I thought you deserved it
I wanted to believe it

Then you stepped too far
Then I couldn't be there
Then I was powerless to help
Then I was unable to be in two places at once

Now I'm despicable
Now my name is dirt
Now a story of my evil is told by you
All for one time I didn't submit to you

Yet I won't give up
I still want to be a hero
I yearn for the doing of good deeds
Even if it's not for you
There's a world of decent people
They deserve my help
I choose them over you

Life's real heroes and villains
Look closely and you'll spot them

The Lies of Perception

Conversations with friends
Conversations turn dark
Friends turn to enemies
Then I awake from sleep

I walk a path
The path stretches before me
I run it with no end or escape
Then I awake from sleep

I hear things not seen
See things no-one notices
Perceive dangers unknown to all
I awaken not from sleep
For I'm already awake

Are things real?
Is my perception honest?
Does reality lie to me?
Or is it my brain?

I might never know
I'll simply carry on living
Don't mind me
Just screaming at nothing

Love Letter of Reality

I love you
I love you in every waking, sleeping moment
I love you in everything
Through everything
Despite everything

I love you when my soul takes flight
I love you when my heart shatters
I love you when you bless me with attention
I love you when shadows fall because you
ignore me

I love you in our long, nightly talks
I love you in the silence of your apathy
I love you when you require me
I love you when I am cast aside in boredom

I love you when you don't love me
I love you when my heart and your behavior
warn me against it
I love you when I remember our time together
I love you even now, since you left me

In life
In death

In loneliness
In everything
In nothing
I will always love you

Childhood Fears, Grown-up Tears

What scared me as a child?
Shadows of darkness
Creepy-crawly critters
Ghosties and ghoulies
Indistinct allusions to the supernatural

Now adulthood sets in
What scares me today?

Nothing
I mean literally nothing
The actual concept of permanent nothingness
I find this terrifying

A life without purpose
No good deeds or achievements
No impact to make
No legacy to leave
Unnoticed and unloved
Now and always
No escape from the nothing void

It makes my soul freeze
The idea alone gives me chills

What if the idea's reality passes?

Nobody will ever know if it does
That's the scariest thing of all

An eternity of never existing